sophia lethe

talks doxodox down

sophia lethe talks doxodox down

A Dialogue by
Robert Savino Oventile & Sandy Florian

atmosphere press

Contents

Sophia Lethe
Talks Doxodox Down

alliteration

D: Sophia, listen.

SL: Doxodox, you know I loathe to listen.

D: Today I think I thought a thought.

SL: Like the skunk who sat on the stump and thought the stump stunk?

D: No, more like the stump upon which the skunk sat who thought the skunk stunk.

SL: Or the imaginary menagerie manager who imagines he manages the imaginary menagerie.

D: No, more like the imaginary menagerie that imagines it is managed by the imaginary menagerie manager.

SL: Let me guess. The thought you thought wasn't the thought you thought you thought.

D: Precisely, because if the thought I thought I thought had been the thought I thought …

SL: It's a slippery slope down that Slip & Slide.

D: I wouldn't have thought so much.

SL: For if thinking validates being …

D: I think not, therefore I am not.

SL: If you only had a brain.

allusion

D: Will said nothing.
SL: To act toward disappearance wills appearance.
D: Make steady eye contact with Janus!
SL: Willy-nilly images the will's persistence.
D: Nihil-I remains a will-I?
SL: Only Jonah would find this a problem.
D: The will ceases, the muse appears.
SL: Ha! A hope for appearance!
D: But: "only pure absence [...] can inspire." So the Algerian wrote.
SL: My inerrant apocalypse, you are impossible.
D: Neither more nor less than ashen letters floating up a chimney and skyward to summon Athena in the guise of a British nanny.
SL: For your sake, Apollo in the guise of a parking meter: the brainchild's fiery, surprising advent may come to pass.
D: So with Paul call the will the heart's foreskin.
SL: Which concedes to me.
D: Willingly.

aposiopesis

D: If I were to tear out my heart, you'd find – But no! Oh no!
Let me say no more about what you would find!
SL: If you were to tear out (finally) –
D: If you were to tear off my arms, you'd see – But foreclose!
Foreclosure! Let me shut my trapdoor!
SL: A veritable Venus de Milo!
D: Or if you were to amputate my feet, no, my calves, no, my
knees, you'd find –
SL: Where your thighs meet your hips?
D: Yes! If you were to circumcise – but oh! The thought
beyond thoughts!
SL: Why not simply cut that line on the wrists? For then you
would see –
D: Don't say what I'd see. For those words are too dark.
SL: Those words too dark for words?
D: So cut at my shoulders, no, at my -
SL: Chim chiminey chim chim cheroo
D: Yes, at my chin, yes, my chin, no – my mou –
SL: The sweep is as lucky –
D & SL: As lucky can be!

anacoluthon

D: May the soul find the dispersion of—yet the heart wished a world.
SL: An old inconsistency.
D: Or a confusion of dispersion for the world's abandonment.
SL: Why not the world's abandon?
D: If the world opened upon the earth—
SL: Answer directly, please.
D: Due to the mirage of another world—
SL: This word world tastes of—but were sensations ever simply of the world?
D: Yet occur nowhere but the world, ergo the heart's wish.

anadiplosis

D: Here let's sing a song. A song with harmony. A song with melody.
SL: Yes let's. About?
D: How the soul becomes a body. How a body becomes dust. How dust becomes blown by wind.
SL: Striking.
D: How in the beginning was the word and the word was with God and the word was—
SL: More striking still.
D: Silence!
SL: Truly striking!
D: I said quiet!
SL: How the word was quiet! How the quiet was endemic. How the endemic became pandemic.
D: No, pandemonium!
SL: This world without form! The form without flute!
D: The flute without song, without harmony, or tune!
SL: Yes let's sing a song!

analogy

D: What the Immaculate Conception was to Mary, the *creatio ex nihilo* was to the deep.
SL: An assistant is to absence's conjuration as a veil is to presence's fabrication.
D: Words are to silence what waves are to wind.
SL: Confound the word in the wave! Chaos breeds song.
D: Just as endlessness spawns thought.
SL: Night distributes change like distraction allows theft.
D: In the beginning, with perfect darkness our only mirror?
SL: For the promised duet, yes.
SL & D: From welter and waste,
   With temper and taste,
   Compound the dust
   With daemons and rust.

anaphora

SL: In you, I find death as if it were alive. In you, I foresee things that are torn in half, that vanish, and are disappeared. In you, devilish affairs are set forth with goals of conquering and captivation.

D: The wish of the genuine magician must be flamboyant.

SL: (. . .)

D: Instead of endeavoring to amuse mankind with the neatness of the concrete world, he must endeavor to improve the world by the power of his concentration.

SL: (. . .)

D: Instead of seeking praise by deceiving the senses of the spectator, he must strive for fame by conquering the supernatural.

SL: *Slowly and grimily we advance through this darkness, not knowing what lies ahead, not knowing what we will find at the end of the path, not knowing that we are so near Disneyland.*

D: Why, if you can get the lantern lit, if you can find the main cave, and if you can see with your eyes open, I'll show you my new bat collection.

SL: Please stroke Sophia very softly, very slowly, very smoothly.

antanagoge

D: The smoothly sibilant [s], the slowly labial [f], the softly given [ə].
SL: And [ō], the [ē], Doxy.
(...)
D: This Mekong evaporating down to its own artifice shows a name lending itself to a second life of perfect sheen.
SL: But in recompense provokes a rage for memory.
D: For justice. For overwhelming texture.
SL: Main Street again.
D: Our tram circles tirelessly, but we passengers begin a journey. Consider that funambulist: each step finely mimics the last yet suggests a gait presently nowhere traversing the lands.
SL: Does this day warrant brooding?
D: Come renovation or ruin, I pledge my heart against this effluent light!
SL: Or: the light flattens out in bravura profiles but not without beckoning shadows.

antimetabole

SL: Before the renovation of the ruin comes the ruination of
the renovation.
D: The preamble to the post-apocalypse.
SL: Before the elimination of memory comes the memory of
the elimination.
D: The codicil to the living will.
SL: Before the end of time comes the time of the end.
D: "Ex nihilo nihil fit."
SL: All I'm pledging for is an orchestra seat, front and center.
D: All I'm pledging for is a Shakespearean finale, tear-ducts,
and a glass of warm milk.
SL: Is it the beginning of the end? or the end of the
beginning?
D: A morning lullaby.
SL: A midnight bugle.
D: Goodnight sunshine.
SL: Goodnight moon.

antiphrasis

D: In the whispers anticipating the wind, I hear nothing.
SL: Then dewax, Your Attentiveness.
D: At the shore, I rush the shell away from my ear.
SL: Stop pretending the cochlea is no shell.
D: Stop pretending far within a tiny hair doesn't dance to the deep without.
SL: Hornpipe to the grandest storm you wish, you remain an ear trumpet to your own sanity.
D: Where but toward sonority should I orient audition?
SL: Listen for a hiatus.
D: Must I pre-imagine the instant when I point to your lips?
SL: How considerate, letting me go first, as if toward your still, gapped lips my forefinger might never direct attention.
D: Stop pretending
SL: Hush—Stop pretending never to stop.

barbarismus

D: Sophia, prey tell, by the pedals of a well-known flour.
SL: Yes, your heinousness?
D: Do you love me? or love me not?
SL: Let's say, in deed, you've piqued my interest.
D: But, Sophia, is it love? I am weighting.
SL: Let's say I regard your meddle and your mite.
D: But Sophia, I weight with baited breath! With rapped attention!
SL: Let's say you are a perfect purl. A perfect pyknic.
D: I rack my brain! I just can't bear it!
SL: Let's say I might be one (alone).
D: Raze Cain! When will I win? I need to know!
SL: Oh Dox. You'll get your just deserts.
D: Hail Mary full of grace!
SL: . . .
D: (I'm a shoe-in.)

bathos

D: You render superfluous quests to justify existence.

SL: I do willingly stand the next round. Chug-a-lug!

D: Where praise can only falter, let silence voice acclaim.

SL: The dryer shrank this dress a bit, don't you think?

D: Onward, in dizzying downward flight, to Creation's verge!

SL: Okay, those stairs may still be manageable.

D: What pavilions, what twilit vistas of greenery!

SL: And there's not much soot on the chaise lounges either side of the lap pool.

D: Let the gods prepare a throne, immaculate, gleaming, pearlescent.

SL: Give it a lick and a promise.

D: My finite parts sink into a trance, yet my thought reaches toward you, a vision in ivory, so near, yet so far.

SL: Look! The robes are monogrammed.

D: Could I rise from this couch and cross to the farther shore, come what mortal haps may! Could I ...

SL: Could you stay awake.

catachresis

SL: Death is so deep, don't you agree?
D: Yes, death is as deep as the crevice on my thimble.
SL: Imagine waking to find death a crevice in your pillow,
nourished by the very air you snore.
D: Yes! Death brings nightmares to my boring corpse.
SL: Stirs the passions in the dull moo cow.
D: Tickles the monkey of the funny bone.
SL: While the inner ear listens for whisperings.
D: Yes, yes, I listen vainly, and with a hungry tum.
SL: No, I am too full for birds. Why my stitch is all unhitched!
D: Why, your lessons are dogs.
SL: Why, you listen with kittens.
D: Let's sing a song, my little hippo.
SL: Yes, let's sing a song, my mighty mouse.

chiasmus

D: Could I breach my dreaming by my dreaming a breach!
SL: But at a threshold, the will demands a dream.
D: Arguing the dream refracts yet bears the liminal.
SL: Still, and again: if rift, then will; if willing, then dreaming on.
D: But in a schism between the dream of the will and the will of the dream, a rift may find a way.
SL: Of what in the Valhalla do you speak?
D: Of the narrowest of passages between sleeping and waking.
SL: Perhaps, if dreaming from an impossible anamorphic angle.
D: Or if the dream became to the will a piece of Iceland spar.
SL: So, tell me dreamily to will myself dreamily to tell you, "Who am I, then, if not your will?"
D: *O ma belle guerrière!*
SL: I will not not will!
D: The breach! The breach!
D & SL: Wind and stars,
       Stars and wind,
       Air warm on skin.

antithesis

D: We walk the deserted path today only to reach the cemetery gates tomorrow.
SL: The world shall remember us not by how well we lived, but how good we looked.
D: Not wrinkled, but pumped virally.
SL: The nip and tuck is one small step for man, one giant leap for stretch-marks.
D: Some men see baldness and say why. I dream of hair plugs and say why not?
SL: I dream of washing that grey right out of my armpits.
D: I dream of stomach staples.
SL: I dream of pealing my face.
D: Yes, because although the surface of your skin appears to be soft-focused, as I don my second-hand tortoise shelled bifocals, it appears cratered instead. Quite moonlike.
SL: Are you saying what I think you're saying?
D: It's not that we love heaven less, but that we hate looking like hell.
SL: Today we observe not the victory over death, but a celebration of surgery.
D: Hurray!

distinctio

SL: Are you ready to talk prostheses?

D: If by "ready" you mean "capable," you tell me. If "despairing of further resistance," then yes.

SL: By "talk," I imply not evasion but articulation.

D: My mood suits an encounter.

SL: What if by "God" dictionaries insinuate: the prosthesis of encounter?

D: Would secrecy then be impossible? Instead of a contradiction to physics or to logic, by "impossible" please understand: an immemorial event.

SL: Your phobia regards memorials?

D: Souvenirs' lurid gossip merely anesthetizes loss.

SL: I'll bite: "Loss": this or that gone, but here: the only sensation harboring a worthy reminiscence.

D: Loss, the only prosthesis to articulate yet guard a secret.

(...)

SL: Let's hope for a return of your extravagant-schemes disposition.

D: Agreed.

apophasis

D: So, are you ready to answer this question about the goodness of God?

SL: Yes, but I must warn you, my dearest Dox, that throughout this descent, I will say nothing to the fact that there's nothing good at all to be said about God.

D: For once, I agree with you, for it's not my habit either to comment on this God whom I dislike, or who, for whatever reason, has granted me two elfin ears, not to mention these two buck teeth through which I lisp.

SL: To say nothing of your Mister Magoo eyes and that horrible blindness of yours!

D: No, we will say nothing in the likes that he is an egotistical bottom feeder, grooming himself off the crops from the ugliest men.

SL: Nor do we have time to list all his felonious offences, or the lurid rumors of his sexual impotence with both virgins and whores.

D: We will not bring up the matter of his spiritual bankruptcy, because other reasons clearly enough show that he's not even worth the words we speak.

SL: Yes, and we must ignore his cheap tricks, his quote-unquote magical enterprises, his ultimately unimpressive invisibility.

D: Like those reruns with Moses and that serpent staff! No, we will definitely not mention the flamboyance of his Freudian chicaneries.

SL: Nor will we suggest that he is solely responsible for the construction of hell!

D: Of course, So, I do not need to mention that you should bring along with you a No. 2 pencil.

SL: Why, Dox, if I didn't like you so, I'd say you were trying to cheat.

epanalepsis

SL: Believe you in the provocations to believe?
D: Hope for discernment argues I must discriminate among hopes.
SL: Hearing you mention hope puts in question my hearing.
D: The absconded aforesaid unmentionable carelessly left behind an exquisitely useful yearning for the absconded.
SL: Before reuse, anything of the aforesaid requires at least bleach.
D: Verily, like an abandoned hypodermic, yet only by reuse might desire undergo redirection.
SL: Risk of infection remains an inevitable risk.
D: Infection by longing leaves the choice to redefine infection.
SL: Perhaps your vocabulary betrays a vestigial symptom.
D: Joyful laughter, too, is infectious.
SL: Joy you in inexistent solicitations to joy?
D: Only if my musical taste can discern among truants.
SL: I do still await your taste's demonstration, I do.

epistrophe

D: How at our heights the bird quill song agonizes my auditory ossicles.

SL: That aerial racket agonizes. This bird-eye panorama agonizes. And that human stench rising from the crowd below forever agonizes my soul.

D: Perhaps we'd be better off descending to the nether parts, mingling with the hoi-polloi.

SL: Up down. Up down. Up down.

D: Perhaps we could learn to live with the hoi-polloi. We could learn to love the hoi-polloi. We could embroider "I HEART THE HOI-POLLOI" on our habiliments.

SL: We were born without "I HEART THE HOI-POLLOI" habiliments. We now live without "I HEART THE HOI-POLLOI" habiliments. We will die without "I HEART THE HOI-POLLOI" habiliments.

D: But if living up here is detestable, if living down there is detestable, where shall we go that is not, dear, detestable?

SL: Truthfully, I admit. Heights we cannot bear. Depths we cannot bear.

D: Are you thinking what I'm thinking!

D & SL: A bottle of booze like a bottle of bees and off the balcony we'll bounce!

aporia

D: Pray tell, my dear Sophia, can virtue be taught?
SL: Why, I am an amnesiac sort of person, Dox, and can't recall even its definition. I recall only that you, my dear Dox, have a wonderful woman's virtue.
D: I know not whether you insult me, or whether you are referring to my most selective qualities—my crisp and dishpan hands, my alphabetized collection of coupon clippings, and my aproned obedience to you. But I aver, I am no eunuch. I am a manly man, a proper man, a raging stallion, a fevered man.
SL: Why, I don't know if by "raging" and "stallion" you are referring to your awful nyctophobia and your unfortunate equestrian proboscis. I don't know if by "fevered," you are referring to your wrinkle of delirium tremens. All know that your mascara is running, your lipstick is smeared, and your excessive use of hairspray is balding your bald-spot.
D: Why, you sting me! You stingray! You number of mind and lips! I don't know whether I should be questioning the decision to be or not to be or whether you should be arrested for your wizardry.
SL: I don't remember whether it's best to be or not to be. I only recall that the virtues of wizards nictate, that they mingle with the virtues of the stars.
D: I am abandoned! I am bereft! Grant me one small relaxation, So, pray tell me, do you still love me in the dark.
SL: Dox, like a star among stars, I only love you in the dark.
D: (...)

epithet

SL: You evergreen fool! Will you never again speak to me of me?

D: To win a title: Virtuous Speaker. Perhaps in defenestration's brief interval.

SL: Couldn't I\you just hit a dropping elevator's red button to grant a moment?

D: In depthless falling, the "of you" avoids flawing the "to you" with "I." To speak with vulgar topicality but without tedious judgment: so flawing speech, the speaker wakes to die, hanging bewigged in Bangkok.

SL: Falling too is an awakening process. Yes, my gruesome logician, one distinct from hanging.

D: Falling, the heart-in-the-throat vertigo of intimate separation.

SL: Of intimate desperation.

D: Consider the interstellar chasms spacing "me" from "I," "me" from "you."

SL: So, "I am me" enforces a burdensome pretense, besides questionable grammar?

D: Confusion seize the anxious pedant! A tragic muse cries out, "O, woe is me!," *not* "O, woe am I!"

SL: Her "me" hosts passions.

D: Of the secrets within me I articulate naught. For me to speak virtuously requires the inspiration of another I.

SL: An inspiration indistinguishable from falling?

D: Suspending volition, falling gives voice to me, to speak to you, of you.

epizeuxis

D: The best way to describe this aerial state is divine, divine, divine!

SL: Yes, yes! Divine, divine!

D: What do you see?

SL: Honey, honey, honey, flowing everywhere, everywhere.

D: Yes, yes. Milk and honey. Milk and honey.

SL: What do you hear?

D: The birds singing rejoice, rejoice, rejoice!

SL: Yes, yes! Rejoice, rejoice, rejoice!

D: What do you smell?

SL: Ambrosia, sweet, sweet, sweet ambrosia.

D: Yes, yes. Sweet ambrosia.

SL: What do you taste?

D: Nectar, nectar, nectar of the gods.

SL: Yes, nectar, nectar.

D: What do you feel?

SL: Sick, sick, sick, sick, sick, sick, sick, sick, sick, sick, sick, sick, sick, sick, sick to my stomach.

D: Me too! Sick, sick, sick.

hyperbaton

SL: Relax, I said, fear of floating Ferris anticipated: every up heralds a down.
D: So we tried to exorcise the only descent.
SL: From the funhouse, me you had followed.
D: A portal for me the darkness and disorientation were.
SL: I remember your eyes wide.
D: Through each iris rushed an expanding horizon, such acreage of treetops!
SL: And the steeple *below* us!
D: And the clock tower only a building to gather buildings around!

eponym

D: Stop forgetting I exist. Your so-called amnesia is starting to look like Alzheimer's, if I do say so myself.

SL: It's Asperger's, not Alzheimer's.

D: Your Alice in Wonderland Syndrome is so Kafkaesque that I predict your avoidance of me will prove to be your Achilles' heel.

SL: I need a cocktail.

D: You need a Meyer's cocktail.

SL: *Ut tensio sic vis.*

D: Why, I would gain more affection if you followed Asimov's Rules of Robotics.

SL: Why, I'd rather be driving my diesel engine all over the atlas taking daguerreotypes.

D: We could settle down and have children! We could name them Murphy, Finagle, and Herblock.

SL: I'd rather make a Ferris wheel of my Fallopian tubes.

D: After all, according to Littlewood's law, I should expect a miracle about once per month.

SL: It always takes longer than you expect, even when you take into account Hofstadter's Law.

D: Would you love me more if I procured a Prince Albert?

SL: I would only love you more if you were a Barbie.

D: Speaking of Mattel Inc., let's follow Reilly's Law of Retail Gravitation and patronize the bigger and better shopping mall on Main.

SL: Only now do you make sense, Doxodox. After all, according to Roemer's Law, a hospital bed built is a hospital bed filled.

litotes

SL: You find this escalator no irrelevancy?
D: The contraption descends patrons not without
ambivalence: is the rider an aristocrat a mechanical litter
parades or only another product a belt conveys?
SL: I just now envisioned your guillotined, boxed head in
single downward procession.
D: As if marching onward yet without feet.
SL: No, no—as if you lived on elsewhere, in the Piedmont, an
acephalous wanderer!
D: A not unmoving vision.
SL: But one not quite limitless. Continue the experiment:
perambulating valleys and hills, why does the wanderer find
nothing unbecoming?
D: Because he crosses an earth wholly without mirrors?
Because each sensation arrives as wisdom?
SL: No and no. Because the wanderer, so not incredulous,
always believed and still believes the cranium hosts what
nothing contains: the timeless, the placeless.

onomatopoeia

SL: Yawn. Sigh. Hiccup.

D: The clock goes tick-tock and all you can do is purr, rattle, and snort.

SL: Cough cough cough. Honk honk honk.

D: Shush up! Muffle yourself. Can't you see I am trying to philosophize? I am trying to practice dying!

SL: Snap snap snap. Clap clap clap.

D: Can you zip it? Can you snip it? Can you squish it?

SL: Groan. Hiss. Growl. Bark bark. Woof woof.

D: I see there's no thumping through that rumble of yours.

SL: Oink. Neigh. Moo. Bark bark. Woof woof.

D: Ring-a-ling! Earth to So!

SL: Ugh, I know, Dox, that the wheels of time clank, clatter, and twang. But it all seems so blah. So bland. So humdrum.

D: Shall I jangle you a joke my little pet? Shall I gurgle you a giggle?

SL: Oh do, Dox. Prey jest.

D: Knock knock.

SL: Who's there?

D: Boo.

SL: Boo hoo?

D: Boo-hoo-hoo-hoo-hoo! [Bonk!] [Thud.] Argh! Ouch! Who turned out the lights?

SL: [Dot dot dot.]

D: Are you there So? Are you with me in this darkness?

SL: Don't cry, Doxodox! I was only joking!

D: Groan.

metanoia

D: Look below: glorying above the glacial valley's mist-veiled darkness, your Brocken Spectre beckons!

SL: Not mine: yours.

D: Colors bright and worthy halo your lithe shadow.

SL: Not mine: yours.

D: This moment will haunt my memory.

SL: My quite hypoxic Dox—listen! You merely confuse our shadows.

D: Merely confuse our shadows? I simply descry my fate!

SL: Your fate? Your quixotically willful error ... You know my shadow's full and ample anticorona will forever remain empty air to your eyes (as your shadow's will to mine ...).

D: Not empty air: a still life only the earth's dun curvature frames.

SL: Not a still life but a potential *tableau mort* with you as the *rücken figure* of the perpetually hidden and beblubbered countenance.

D: Where's my camera?

SL: Embrace the moment? No: you'd rather skip right to its memorialization, its memento morialization, its marmorealization ...

D: The marmalade orange achingly glows. Is my camera in your pack?

SL: Wrestling error together, descending together, we could meditate on the empty air together.

D: I know: let's dump both packs out onto the snow.

SL: Enough! I'm heading down.

personification

D: Oh how heavy is my heart.
SF: Perhaps you should put your heart on a diet.
D: How it cries for the tragedy of life.
SF: Debark it by stretching its vocal chords.
D: How it withers like an autumn leaf reaching its tendrils toward winter.
SF: Give it a face-lift, a tummy tuck, a transplant.
D: How it tires, Sophia, of your lack of nurture.
SF: It is not nature's position to nurture.
D: How my words try to make you understand.
SF: How your words fail to water even the swimming pool.
D: Okay. From now on, Sophia, I am only going to speak to you from my heart.
SF: The old heart to heart? You don't say. I mean, of course, your heart doesn't say.
D: Yes. My heart is going to speak to your heart, whether your heart is a heart of sickness, whether your heart is a heart of madness, whether your heart is a heart of derangement. Whatever your heart may be, henceforth, only my heart will speak to your heart and to your heart my heart will speak only.
SF: Okay, Doxodox. You win. My heart is listening.
D: Hold your horses. My heart is thinking.
SF: Your heart is thinking. But my heart is waiting.
D: Your heart is waiting. But my heart is contemplating.
SF: Your heart is contemplating. But my heart is growing impatient.
D: Your heart is growing impatient, Sophia. But my heart can't get this stupid song out its head.
SF: [?]
D: [. . .]
SF: [!]

D: Did you happen to see the most beautiful girl in the world?

SF: And if you did, was she crying, cry-ing?

D & SF: Hey, if you happen to see the most beautiful girl that walked out on me—

La la la la . . . la . . . la . . . laaaa

pleonasm

SL: So you do believe in the mutely inarticulate?

D: Yes, in a clandestine secret, the taciturn fount of all our verbose wordiness whatsoever.

SL: A secret between us, you and me?

D: Ours solely alone, a single powdery gray ash somehow foliating innumerable burning colorful flames: orange, red, and yellow.

SL: You assume our entanglement in an extravagantly plotted scheme.

D: No, in a lucky event of fateful chance.

SL: Now you believe in a contradiction: "fateful chance"?!??!!

D: A surprising, unforeseeable rearranging of my every star, each glimmering point.

SL: Energized a minute subatomic bit, the roundish orbitals of your tiny electrons undergo unprecedented vibrations.

D: Indeed, well said.

SL: Then tell me verbally with your own speaking voice this confidential hush-hush.

D: By my redundant name, my every word guards

SL: Maybe, perhaps, just this time, for once, try on this contradiction: passion for a secret demands its betrayal in utterance.

D: Because any attempt at articulation only further enacts the inexorable burial in impenetrable secrecy?

SL: No, because where you actually betray belief is in your unguarded hope a secret could be ours together at all without being anyone's.

non-sequitur

D: It is not nature's nature to nurture. It is human beings' nature to nurture. Therefore, human beings are not part of nature.

SL: Human beings have arms and legs. Supermen have arms and legs. Therefore, human beings are supermen.

SL: Superman lives in Hollywood. Superwoman lives in Hollywood. Therefore, Superman and Superwoman live together.

D: The climate in Hollywood is very hot. The climate in hell is very hot. Therefore, Hollywood is hell.

SL: Superman and Superwoman live in hell. Only sinners live in hell. Therefore, Superman and Superwoman are mortal sinners.

D: Hell is hilly. Hell has no public transportation. Therefore, you need a car to live in hell.

SL: I'm thinking Cadillac. What are you thinking?

D: I'm thinking Rolls Royce.

querimonia

SL: Again you've misplaced your horn-rims?
D: In the limo ... The phone booth? Somewhere in Hollywood
... Would you
SL: First I have to help you find your vision. Then I have to
help you find your vision.
D: Well, if you'd simply let me keep a pair here
SL: Your distraction results, I charge, from your living as if in
a rerun flickering on a mausoleum wall.
D: I cannot read this accursed phone number. Please
SL: Always gawking skyward while fumbling in the
foreground.
D: Maybe in the cemetery ...
SL: Your aviators you never lose. Think on that.
D: Help me remember what, where
SL: You know memory's not my gift, not to you. Or does your
resolve waver?
D: No. And you know I'm training to see in diminishing light.
SL: In the interminable meantime, just glance down next to
the keyboard.
D: Oh. Thanks.

understatement

D: Our fall from that 10th story window did result in a couple of scrapes, wouldn't you say?

SL: Why yes. It seems we're just a tad flayed around the edges.

D: Yes, I wouldn't have foreseen how much shelling the skin from the face alters the visage.

SL: It does blur things a bit, I agree. But I think we'll look as good as new with just a little mascara. Especially after we reinsert our eyes.

D: Of course, of course. By the way, Sophia, do you mind passing me my arm laying by your feet over there? It seems I'm a bit shorthanded at the moment.

SL: My pleasure, Doxodox. Let me just first wipe these entrails from my mouth. It seems I might be suffering from a little nausea.

D: No problem. Here, why don't you use this rag to wipe it clean.

SL: Silly bird. That's not a rag. That's your scalp. I hope you're not in terrible pain over this.

D: Not at all. Not at all. I'm just a little sore. You?

SL: Oh, it stings a bit here and there. But I'll be fine.

D: Why look who's here. If it isn't the Grim Reaper.

SL: The Grim Reaper, eh? Well that does cast a small gloom over this short evening, doesn't it?

D: Just a bit, So. Just a bit.

restrictio

D: Who knew the clinic offers luxury rooms nowhere but in the basement?
SL: A room with every amenity, just no windows.
D: There's no discerning the hour without looking at the clock.
SL: Which you laboriously unplugged, along with the TV.
D: While I could. These straps allow no movement save to boost the morphine.
SL: Excluding our chatter, there's no sound here. Nothing to feel but pain dulled.
D: No smells but the antiseptics. Nothing to see but a blank ceiling.
SL: I can move everything barring my head, neck, shoulders, arms, hands, torso, hips, legs, and feet.
D: There's nothing to do.
SL: Except to tell our dreams.
D: I dreamt I knew death was anything but a release.
SL: I dreamt you knew only reflections yet sought nothing but my voice.
D: I dreamt every silence will echo yours.
SL: I dreamt our words will bring down rain.

parallelism

D: Savage animals devouring flesh and fiendish wizards hexing spells practice evil by night in this, our motel of darkness.

SL: Malevolent spirits consuming death and diabolical demons possessing spirits enslave us in this, our hotel of gloom.

D: While nurses walk down the stairwell, through the doors, and into our chambers singing, "Up, up, and away."

SL: And doctors walk up the stairwell, through the doors, and into our chambers chiming, "In my beautiful balloon."

D: Claiming they have great skill in optics and instructing us to look more lovingly at these shadows on the wall.

SL: Maintaining that they are experts in neurology and insisting that we retrain our brains to regard with more affection these monsters and goblins.

D: "Up, up, and away."

SL: "In my beautiful balloon."

D: "The world's a nicer place."

SL: "In my beautiful balloon."

D: But I'd spare my eyes for a pair of exits.

SL: I'd spare mouth for an underground tunnel.

D: My lone left elbow for a finger of liberty.

SL: My beating heart for a single chance.

D: A chance?

SL: Yes, a chance. A chance on Broadway, baby.

D: On Broadway.

tricolon

SL: I will hum, I will tap, I will act! Search out a script, a curious scenario, a quietly haunting *mise en scène*!

D: Ponder a stark kabuki: A felt robe lounges on a mat; a silk kimono sways from a hook; a gliding wall opens onto nightfall.

SL: You see how my mouth yawns.

D: The frozen face of the deep, motionless arctic air and polar darkness encircle a Styrofoam igloo from which glowing notes stream.

SL: More urban, less wary, even unruly.

D: At a backlit trolley stop, office-tower gusts sculpt me your absence from a chaos of leaves.

SL: Or consider a cross-costumed farce: you brood in *la casita*; I carouse across *la ciudad*; the Gulf of Mexico beckons toward *el horizonte*.

D: With a broken tower? With a mime troupe of sharks? With a great *papier-mâché* propeller shredding a tinsel sea?

SL: I see how your eyes flinch.

synecdoche

SL: Doxodox? Can you lend me a hand?
D: I'm all ears, Sophia.
SL: Keep your eye on my slot machine while I belly up to the bar.
D: I'd love to So, but I'm all fingers and thumbs at the moment.
SL: What? You can't get a handle on your handle?
D: I keep hitting the duds.
SL: You know what we need, Doxodox?
D: No, So. What do we need?
SL: A couple of hired hands.
D: Yes, and a hundred head of cattle.
SL: Why, if we had some greenbacks, we could get us some wheels, put on our best threads, and burn rubber down the strip.
D: We could pay, not pray, for our daily bread.
SL: I'd say. You do have some mouth to feed.
D: I hunger only for your love!
SL: In that, my dear, you need to get your head examined.
D: Perhaps. But I should start first by finding my legs at this slot.
SL: It's tough to win a buck these days.
D: We should have been a pair of padded paws.
SL: Whiskers and Boots?
D: Boots and Whiskers.

synzeugma

D: Each billboard we escaped and every prediction.
SL: Across state lines our delight flew and across time zones.
D: Dusk from night I could distinguish, living from living on.
SL: Of a devil Mademoiselle gracing a float you mused and of an ember-eyed zombie lurching through Storyville.
D: Of a yellow fleur-de-lis you sang and of a dancing fullness.
SL: Through trombones a pleasing languor spoke and through clarinets.
D: Past misnomers you led me and away from embalmment.
SL: Monuments I evaded and erasure.
D: To veracity's border you beckoned and to articulation's edge.
SL: Toward our rendezvous we sped, toward our end.

sententia

D: A penny for your thoughts.
SL: In for a penny, in for a pound.
D: But a penny saved is a penny earned.
SL: The more you pay the more it's worth.
D: Have it your way. A pound. A pound for your thoughts.
SL: Let the buyer beware.
D: Let the chips fall where they may.
SL: Deal. I slept and dreamt that life was Beauty. I awoke and found that life was Duty. That's life, I suppose. Some days it just doesn't pay to get out of bed.
D: Aww, pucker up, butter cup. Reality bites, but time heals all wounds. So put your best foot forward. Put your nose to the grindstone. Put your shoulder to the wheel. Someday our ship will come.
SL: [Like the blind leading the blind.]
D: [There's none so blind as those who will not see.]
SL: [Seeing is believing. But it's what you don't see that matters. That a fool and his money are soon departed.] So put your money where your mouth is. Put up or shut up. Show me the money. And don't quit your day job.
D: Egads! Fine! Take your money and run.
SL: [Another day, another dollar.]

parataxis

D: Reject common ground. Let's be contiguous.
SL: Nothing escapes exchange. There's always a corpus callosum.
D: Must bridges coordinate and subordinate? My style must change.
SL: Yoking harbors ambivalence. "Best safety lies in fear."
D: Must hinges imply locks? There's no sin below the equator.
SL: Clouds teach thought well. Thrones in the lovely blueness are nonsense.
D: A scrap backs the collage. Houses sacrifice Mercutio to order.
SL: My upwelling is no ideal object. Extravagance demands resolve.
D: I would love my fate. Sometimes goldfish outlive all expectations.

enthymeme

D: We pass away, for we exist.
SL: Ripples on a stream, racks in a breeze.
D: Porous to sense, for we breathe.
SL: Wondrously receptive sponges!
D: Without belief, for we think.
SL: You believe logic captivates me …
D: If the thoughtless did offend, then the thoughtful will please.
SL: Reason hesitates. You reason.
D: All talk reasons. So I'm reasoning.
SL: To mark a path, to keep in view a way back.
D: Back to where?
SL: No, back from me.
D: If there's a "from you," then there's a "to you."
SL: "To" and "from" imply distance. You keep your distance.
D: Steps overcome distance. Let's take steps.
SL: The hill is with the valley, for they are distinct.
D: I don't follow.
SL: If distinction joins, then only in a gateway do to and fro go missing.
D: Our feet will wander, for the earth's a threshold?
SL: Let's get well and truly lost.

hendiadys

SL: I am really and truly sick and tired of your huffing and puffing about the weather.
D: But the heat and flame of hell are scorching.
SL: Perhaps if you considered it less fire and brimstone and more tropical, more nice and warm, you'd be more comfortable.
D: Nice and warm? You're good and mad.
SL: It is, after all, raining cats and dogs here and there.
D: Cats and dogs of wrath and fire!
SL: Still, the long and short of it is, we'll be here forever and ever.
D: Forever and a day.
SL: So consider the pros and cons.
D: Pros?
SL: Consider our knowledge of good and evil.
D: Well, yes, that's all fine and good, but what are the pros?
SL: The eternal blush of our arms and legs.
D: Our gold and brown? Our tawny hue?
SL: After all, if we have to live here forever and ever . . .
D: Forever and ever and another day . . .
SL: We might as well get good and tan.
D: That is a fact both tried and true.

ignoratio elenchi

D: Wherever I turn blazes red.
SL: Then refute the redness.
D: In my day, I saw colors.
SL: Granted.
D: In my day, red was a color.
SL: Certainly.
D: Thus red was mine to see.
SL: Try again.
D: Colors imply vision. Red is a color. Presto! My vision endures.
SL: You really must let the argument take hold of you.
D: Every sight I shadow. Redness is a sight. Therefore redness depends on my shadow.
SL: Colors soak in regardless. Red's a color, so allow me to remove your rose-colored glasses.
D: The redness becoming almost a texture cannot be worrisome because my thoughts gain utmost dexterity.
SL: Let a thousand roses bloom. The cup now brimming with wine once stood crimson in a kiln. So why not touch this burning coal to your lips?

scesis onomaton

SL: Here comes a man.

D: A man enduring in enmity, cunning in counsel, wicked in discourse, ugly in gesture.

SL: A man laden with baseness, bereft of virtue, calamitous at the core, why, the father of the fall.

D: Sinful by nature, evildoer, hellion, whoremonger, soul cropper.

SL: Hater of humanity, hater of all creation, spreader of corruption, wreaker of worlds!

D: Here he comes! Prince of Darkness, Beelzebub, Lucifer, The Horned One!

SL: Oh, wait. That's not the devil. That's our waiter.

D & SL: Two gin fizzes, please.

D & SL: Thanks.

synoeciosis

D: Seeking the horizon, a spray of swifts curves skyward.
SL: As if arcing your very center.
D: My vacuum, you mean.
SL: Where you offer fullness welcome.
D: Then why do I exude inhospitality?
SL: To refuse the portraits FedEx hourly attempts to deliver.
D: And thus to accept nothing and no one I have ever divined!
SL: Ahem. *Ahem.*
D: Where sin's damnation prospers, salvation's grace abounds!
SL: Wisdom does crown with glory the mulish chaser of Folly.
D: Only unmockable perishing awakens unmockable
SL: Just sniff this brick-red cab. Sip.
D: A complex, airy attack coupled with a simple, earthy finish.
SL: Amid the wind's rustlings, silences float-dance down.

simile

SL: After such long exposure to the sun, your legs are like pieces of overcooked bacon.
D: The soul in the burned body is like a bird in a burned cage.
SL: And yet you remain constantly attentive to the sun, like a sunflower that turns and turns.
D: Melting.
SL: Like wax.
D: Waxing.
SL: Like the body.
D: Like the wicked who perish before God.
SL: The brighter the goodness, the more easily we melt.
D: Like butter.
SL: Baking, in bacon fat.

topothesia

D: There is a place where names become lost.
SL: There is?
D: Where fingertips absorb copper's texture like pungent smoke.
SL: And common nouns linger?
D: Where waters sheet down blank stone.
SL: Where no verb need hide its irreversible action?
D: Where breath sounds only the gathering and dispersal of pressure.
SL: And the adverbs?
D: Slowly, softly, and gently become palinodes.
SL: Adjectives tarry briefly then yield to contraries.
D: Where reflection remains unknown.
SL: There must be much shade and much quiet.
D: Among marble domes and tall cypress.

procatalepsis

D: Some may say that those palaces of palinodes please more than these palaces of perdition, but we know best that the best and most pleasant palaces are those you can fondle.
SL: True.
D: Of course, you know this to be true, so why do I point it out? Your eyes are on those domes, but your fists find only brimstone.
SL: And fire.
D: And while it's usually argued that the genesis of utopian metropolises lies in the mere dreaming of their swift streets, we both know that, try as we might, we shall not imagine our way out of this labyrinth.
SL: After all . . .
D: Yes, after all, who needs to dream of swift streets when we can instead lie dormant in our dread? I, for one, find solace behind my eyelids. Upon the palindromes of cypress and the shade of nebulous fog.
SL: And it's difficult . . .
D: Yes, it's difficult to see how the pilots of our imaginariums are immune to our concrete realities, it's also easy to understand that these same pilots will someday pay the price of our perdition.
SL: As they plunge into the concrete sidewalk.
D: As they plunge into our concrete world.

palindrome

SL: "I"? Sin is "I"?

D: Eve? No sin is on Eve?

SL: Now live I, ere here I evil won.

D: Ere we were?

SL: Til, adrowse, noontime did emit no one's word alit.

D: 'Tis da Logos ("Reifier"); so go lad, sit!

SL: St. Rosy bees we stone, not sew, see, by sorts.

D: To not: in real roods' civics do, or learn I to, not.

SL: Semes' e-ports, doom's grey-ergs moods trope semes.

D: "Rag icon, eh, cinder, red niche? No cigar!"?

SL: No, evil sememes live on.

D: Seities?

SL: Non.

metonymy

SL: Regard the smiley "i" on the "Merci" of our bill.
D: Hey, Dallas won the game 221 to 0 . . .
SL: Why, our waiter thinks he writes a fine hand . . .
D: . . . and Exxon hiked its prices to $300 a barrel.
SL: . . . believing that his pen is mightier than his service.
D: Wall Street's in a tumult . . .
SL: Still that BLT is still waiting for his Cola.
D: . . . and the White House called the Vatican lukewarm.
SL: Still that wig is waiting for her Pinot.
D: Oh look! A smiley on the Merci!
SL: Oh look! Shrek won the Box Office!
D: I, for one, smile upon our server's blue jeans.
SL: And I, for one, frown upon The Times.

oxymoron

SL: Doxodox, my little ogre, would you be so terribly good as to pass me the fat-free half and half?

D: It would be my joyful trouble. Shall I drop a gallon in your decaf coffee?

SL: That would be wickedly nice. Devilishly kind of you. Do you know what else, Dox, would add an essential luxury to our midnight tea?

D: Some bitter sweet? Some good bad luck?

SL: No, no, my giant dwarf.

D: How about some misanthropic humanitarianism?

SL: No, no, my hellish angel. What we need is a good long squirt from a plastic lemon on our oven-fried oysters!

D: Once again you have revealed the obvious secret. But I have a confident fear it would require a quick road-trip to the 24-hour 7/11, for our pantry is almost empty.

SL: Have we no artificial tree growing on our artificial grass?

D: Nope.

SL: Have we no all-natural artificial flavoring?

D: Not a stitch.

SL: What about some sugarless candy? What about some dark white chocolate?

D: My little problem, if we could be in our pantry, we would be alone together.

SL & D: . . .

SL: I suppose we can have only false hope for a peasant's paradise . . .

D: . . . while we wait patiently for eternal life.

SL: For we were born with these plastic silver spoons in our muted mouths . . .

D: . . . to muffle our softly spoken quiet riots.

metaphor

D: My, how that flatfoot was boiling mad. Can you believe
how he grilled us?
SL: I knew we were cooked when he showed us his radar.
SL: I knew we were fried when he handed us the ticket.
D: Basting him with flattery didn't do the job.
SL: No, that was a mere recipe for disaster.
D: Now we're in a pickle . . .
SL: that's very hard to swallow.
D: Do you feel a singe of repentance? My So, my so-so So?
SL: Not at all. Not at all.
D: Let's keep our eyes peeled . . .
SL: . . . and put the pedal to the metal.

polyptoton

SL: That's it, drive with your eyes exclusively eyeing the rearview mirror, an eye for all the inverse and has been.
D: Just know your skull-taps tapping the code (one tap–floor it! etcetera) may tap into my taste for control, for controlled movement, for controlling purposes.
SL: You track the sun in the circle of chrome. I'll be tracking the silver orb's track up into the trackless, diamond-strewn velvet.
[…]
D: As in the past, some desert miles back, time passes passing well.
SL: Blank black yet?
D: Almost.
SL: I glimpsed your face earlier, tightening into a mask within that tight circumference insatiable for light.
D: Therefore you know for me embalmment knows no attraction, known or unknown.
SL: Cremation seems just as arrogant, with its will to incinerate to cinders.
D: And unfortunately feeds the hope to eclipse Fortune from our fortunes.
SL: And I imagine is just as unimaginative. For the imagination, that is.
D: Yes, the topic bears solely on the topping of *topoi*.
SL: Meteor. A meteoric option flashes across my meteorite.
D: You're the driver.
SL: To ride a roadster racing under moonlight down a road to the sea.

hypophora

D: But when you boil it down, what kind of life do we want? Not the pleasures of Paxil. Not the paradise of Prozac. What we want is the kind of life that makes the serotonin syndrome the standard.
SL: For when you add it all up, what kind of life does that mean? Not the inequities of dopamine. Not the distractions of monoamine. What we want is the kind of life that makes medicinal marijuana legal.
D: Because when reality sets in with its despair and its melancholy, what do we want to do? We want to sit in our lazy chairs and toke.
SL: And when panic sets in with its fear and immobility, how do we resist? We resist it by turning the channels on our remote controls.
D: And when we start surfing the television for the perfect commercial, what do we end up watching?
SL: I don't know Dox, what do we watch?
D: Ask any mermaid you happen to see . . .
SL& D: what's the best tuna? Chicken of the Sea!

synchysis

D: I the sand do relish or the breeze or the bonfire more or the phlegmatic sea the most?

SL: Pungent and grey float the smoke and the whales.

D: The sparkles in the air join the glitters in my eyes.

SL: Just stay lounging you melancholic, or over topple, since neither your shirt, without a collar, nor this scene, or even sleeves, can I believe.

D: I know! Gothic and on a floating stage, acoustic and just off shore ...

SL: The harpist with the ostrich-skin boots and black-feather boa, I must say ...

D: I, when the platform angles a bit, nice touch, just can make out the meadow, vibrantly sanguine, starred with flowers, the carpet depicts, if I squint. A bone pile elevates the drum kit.

SL: I listen and sway, rapt and rhythmic.

D: Silent and null sound the quartet and the instruments. Is this what Homeric dumb show red-eyed for seven hundred and twenty-three miles drove I to witness past innumerable *descansos* if my ears indeed someone did not into sneak wax?

SL: Paranoid and choleric, you speculate and complain. An enchanting musical interlude, more like, from a *commedia dell'arte* improvised with delight.

D: This soundlessness, the tense air, the crows ...

SL: A mask you need wax's opposite to open yourself entire ears blushing fans surging the notes ...

D: ... why I am for I know not how wading forward to orient audition resolution wells up irresistibly Ishmael walks seaward ...

SL: ... alit and aloft mingle tablets and cell phones ...

parenthesis

SL: Freud discovered the three structures of the psyche (the id, the ego, and the superego).

D: Jung believed that individualization could be achieved by the integration of the opposing parts of the psyche (the conscious and the unconscious).

SL: Lacan argued that the unconscious is not a primitive (or archetypal) part of the psyche separate from the conscious (or ego), but rather a complex part of the psyche equally sophisticated.

D: Skinner became an atheist after his teacher (a liberal Christian) tried to assuage his fear of the Hell that his grandmother installed.

SL: I (for one) would prefer the fear of this hell to the promise of that heaven. (Bat-bat-bat.)

D: I (for one) would prefer it if you stopped batting your eyes at the devil (and every Tom, Dick, and Harry to boot) in this hot pen.

SL: Why, I deny batting my eyes (bat-bat-bat) (and who said anything about Tom?).

D: We weep (all three), we weep (just me, myself, and I).

exclamatio

D: Have we run out of tissues already? Curses!
SL: I told you never to rush packing—ever!
D: I know how to stuff a suitcase; don't you deny it!
SL: For these temperatures, who packs only spandex? Who?!?!
D: At least I did not insist on powdered wigs!
SL: We did not need sleep-masks for this darkness visible!
D: Ok, what about you bringing your mail order scrimshaw kit? You ... have ... never ... been ... A WHALER!
SL: Who claimed to be orphic? "Don't worry," you said. "If need be, I can sing us free," you said. And yet, here we are!
D: And what do you do here? You surf channels, each more snowy and blaring than the last!
SL: Maybe if we had less quiet, maybe if someone finally spoke up, a change would come!
D: [...]
SL: Hades is getting to us.
D: You think? Good night!

period

SL: Dox, oh, Dox, while you snoozed, while the stars grossly gaped on, when magnitude became crucial, your very neighbor demoted Pluto.

D: Down then, out then: all gaudy simulacra, without number or birth, must flit away.

SL: Pour a baroque oratorio into your ears, burst a purple grape on your palate, and your mood will clot.

D: Without reserve, the saturnine I hail.

SL: Though sprawled on a dun futon pronouncing yourself leaden, you I doubt.

D: Though, bereft of myself, I have topped off buckets, me you doubt?

SL: If the scale of our brevity were to intrude on you, or if for an instant you kenned the fathomless oblivion rolling toward us, you would truly sit beside the saddle.

D: On the contrary, since the realization happens very strictly *in situ*, by way of some contingency, say a pencil's breakage, my response, no less *in situ*, could only deepen my engagement.

SL: Yet, in his weepy delay, in his melancholy hesitation before accepting Athena's desire, we see Achilles disengage. And, since Athena's desire remains his own deepest wish, we see an Achilles divided.

D: Though fleet time's ambiguous cues and miscues bring me oft to stand, and more often to stumble, and though my self rejects yet returns incessantly to the frets whose peculiar confluences and divergences define nothing less than my self, in these risings and fallings, these comings and goings, no one acts but I.

SL: Only upon your arrival at a place never quite found, though any journey there remains irreversible, and only as re-worded in a language you hear but do not speak (*"Je est un autre!"*), could your boast hold.

D: If there is a mute conductor, giving me over to myself while I am unaware, let me never again say "I."

SL: Notwithstanding your dread, and whatever evasions about "me," "myself," and "I" you attempt, all three a single oboe intones.

D: To have nowhere else to go, nothing else to do, and no one else to be: these creeds I uphold.

SL: In you, hopes for the unavoidable and the unattainable converge.

D: That life admits alternatives, that alternatives beget succor, that succor awaits: these heresies I refuse.

SL: In the place you seek blow winds nothing and no one except a fiction can endure.

D: To come to this place, should I prove willing, what must I perform?

SL: An act without sequel in a moment without future: that is all I ask.

ellipsis

D: I dreamt the clouds were high and scudding, the birds silent and floating, the shadows dark and darkening.
SL: Onto the horse and into the distance! My heart dismisses sadness, my head, gravity.
D: When you pass through, no one can pin you down, no one can call you back.
SL: Myself in harmony with the harpsichord's glee, I welcome surfaces and they, me.
D: An aria may be melodious, a dance graceful, and an oration eloquent.
SL: My ears are open, my eyes quick, and my thoughts eager.
D: Toward some sensations, I am partial, toward others, impartial.
SL: The partial sensations become vessels of glory, the impartial, of dreams.
D: The vessels themselves become glorious, the dreams, textured.
SL: The glory becomes sublime,
D: and the texture, beautiful.
SL: Time for you and I to trip the light fantastic ...
D: ... as the blue ...
SL: ... turns a finer ...
SL & D: ... shade of pale!

symploce

D: Much of what I assert might sound like nonsense, but it's the truth. Much of what I assert might sound like malarkey, but it's the truth. Much of what I assert might sound like balderdash, but it's the truth.
SL: And you are asserting what? And you are repeating what?
D: That you don't want the truth. That you don't believe in truth. That you deplore the truth.
SL: About that you lie. I have nothing against the truth. I have not seen the truth. I have no feelings, true or false, about the truth.
D: Then tell me that you love me. Then tell me that you adore me. Then tell me that you can't live without me.
SL: I cannot begin to love you. I cannot see how I can ever love you. I cannot recommend anyone else to love you.
D: I can't stand it! I can't believe it! I can't listen to it!
SL: The more you uphold your fictions, the merrier you will be. The more you forget your problems, the merrier you will be. The more you drink gin fizzes, the merrier you will be.
D: Excuse me, garcon. Twelve gin fizzes, please.
SL & D: . . .
D: I said twelve! I mean twelve! I want twelve! Bring me twelve!
SL: [Sigh.]

hydrographia

SL: Why hopelessly?
D: Because a drop raised up from another's fall soon falls.
SL: Why helplessly?
D: Because gravity reigns.
SL: Why eternally?
D: Because the smooth wavelets' expanding circles suggest perfection.
SL: Why deeply?
D: Because the dripping piano notes lend an elegiac tone.
SL: Why utterly?
D: Because only air and tension linger a drop on the surface.
SL: Why ardently?
D: Because of the turbulence within each drop.
SL: Why not hopefully?
D: Because the arrow of time favors flat stillness.
SL: Why not helpfully?
D: Because, falling or raised up or at its apogee, a drop forms a convex mirror.
SL: Why not briefly?
D: Because a drop's spherical moment nears innumerable frames per second.
SL: Why not shallowly?
D: Because the falling aches with grace.
SL: Why not scarcely?
D: Because, given commencement, the process goes to completion.
SL: Why not bathetically?
D: Why not indeed?

expletive

SL: All truth is not, in fact, truthful.
D: Much truth, you see, is often fanciful.
SL: The strength of truthfulness, you understand, relies on our desire for accuracy.
D: No one, to be sure, desires to live without accuracy.
SL: Although accuracy is often, in effect, overruled by the imagination.
D: No one, to be sure, desires to live without imagination.
SL: The imagination will survive, we should hope, the very trials of accuracy.
D: We would like, in other words, to be taken on a strange journey.
SL: That, your honor, is the honest truth.
D: The whole truth, if we may, and nothing but the truth.

paradox

D: The guidebook says, "Listen for the silence."
SL: I read pitch darkness gilds the surface with a pleasing radiance.
D: I should bring a camera. Listen to this: "Wonderfully odorous, the attendant mists immediately anesthetize the olfactory nerves."
SL: The back cover boasts, "A taste unlike anything you will ever remember!"
D: Wait, here's a disclaimer: "The bracing cold exposed skin will register in no way gives an indication of the waterway but arrives from the desert of ice and snow just beyond, a perennially favorite attraction closed to visitors in perpetuity."
SL: Go anyway?
D: You bet.

metalepsis

D: Were these the lashes that, batting in the deep, cued a creation ripe for ending?
SL: Only if this was the flashing forth that set the fruit swelling.
D: Was this the chaos that gave credence to Leviathan?
SL: Only if this was the wind that taught the preacher wisdom.
D: Were these the blessed divisions that brought abundance to the pyramids?
SL: Only if you never took this dark cave for pallid death.

metabasis

D: The matters we have been discussing are horrible and grievous, and those that we shall now discuss are wonderful and joyous.

SL: We have spoken only of our sad adversities, and we shall now speak only of our happy prosperity.

D: Thus far, we have spoken only with vulgar controversy, and we shall now only speak with harmonious discourse.

SL: Our dialogues have been wrought with the harsh speech of rhetoric, and now we shall move from hard speech to soft poetry.

D: One might believe it to be too late for a change of tongue, but we will now prove we can move from forked to tuned.

SL: They have already heard our promises, and now we will show them how we perform.

D: Since we have thoroughly convinced them with our performance, henceforth we expect only hardy applause.

thaumasmus

SL: When the low sun looks toward the moon
D: And stars curve the night,
SL: Through the town gate we will step and across the hills
D: To find where the earth meets the sky.
SL: Crying out our wonder, we will push through the veil—
D: All before and afar
SL: Will be blank orbs, wheels within wheels,
D: And vast arcs of fire, and scud, and light.

exemplum

D: I like to dream beyond the drab. For example, today, I would like to wear your pink tutu with sequins.

SL: I suggest you wear something more intelligible. You could don, for instance, your flannel pajamas with the fig leaf embroidery.

D: My flannel pajamas can be verifiably roasting if the weather is warm. Case in point, on a day like today when it's hotter than hell where we are here in hell, they make me ooze in sweating exudation.

SL: It's true that your exudations could be beautifully exorbitant. I notice that when you attempt a spin on the elliptical, for instance, your beads resemble bubbles of moonstone.

D: Your flattery is the palaver of those snub-nosed rhetoricians. As when you say that my bulbs shine like moonstone, I understand that, by subtext, you intend to say I am mephitic.

SL: Flamboyant. But on certain days, I agree that you should wear something more botanical. For example, today, you should wear my pink tutu with sequins.

D: We do well to agree. As, when we resemble one another in the mirror of life, we find in each other's eyes tiny versions of ourselves.

SL: In purples and pinks? In tutus and sequins?

D: Precisely.

SL: As perfect.

hyperbole

SL: Deary, do be a gentleman and deliver me over this looming puddle. It stinks like the river Styx in our deserted midst.

D: Darling, your body weighs planets! My enervated armpits couldn't manage one of your varicose veins.

SL: But my figure is feathery! Not unlike the silk spun from silkworms. And you have the might of Hercules, I might add.

D: Your heft interferes with the moon-tides! It frustrates the friction between the continental plates!

SL: Well, at least, my armpits don't stink. Your body odor interferes with radio transmissions.

D: Your visage offends Pluto! Your hideousness degrades the solar system!

SL: Your weakness shrinks earthworms! Your rudeness cripples paraplegics!

D: Your mass reverses the Big Bang. Perhaps it caused the Big Bang! It severs space and dissolves time!

SL: Severs space? Dissolves time? Are you saying I'm postmodern? That I'm the poster girl of pomo?

D: Magnificently!

SL: Thank you!

D: You're welcome!

accismus

D: Whether you don my fedora concerns me not a wit.
SL: Does it have a rakish look to it? I hadn't noticed.
D: How your dark locks might tumble down, I have never
even thought to consider.
SL: Should I shift the *chapeau* just so.
D: To everything there's an art. And there, on the Florentine
credenza ...
SL: I couldn't possibly reach.
D: Whatever.
SL: I really shouldn't have another.
D: No. Me neither. No.
SL: Anyway, to reach with comfort, I'd have to undo these,
which I just can't see doing. Can you?
D: I see no reason why you should lower the blinds now.

allegory

SL: To know life's mirror, we should study its pupils.
D: I see two alone.
SL: As do I, amidst all the teeming world.
D: These pupils seem to study each other.
SL: Pupils should look to know things, and the mirror offers all things.
D: Twilight, a turbulent sky with clouds, a full-arched rainbow from the east heralding the brief yet lightening-strewn tempest arriving from the west.
SL: No, pupils should know themselves.
D: These pupils, so intent on each other, know nothing the mirror holds.
SL: Perhaps they know their very cores.
D: About them the bow arcs, the storm bursts, yet they observe no weather at all.
SL: Perhaps they observe the eye of the storm or imagine the arc's center point.
D: No, they observe nothing! The mirror has lost their attention. O, thou *False Mirror*!
SL: Calm now, envision calm, focus on the calm; color your thoughts with promise. I promise, look into me: I will look back into you.

protherapeia

SL: Remoteness can enchant, but a frozen isle floating in the Laptev Sea?

D: Here noon reveals indigo and hides shadows from shamans.

SL: I appreciate your fondness for oddities; still, what an unusual aperture ...

D: Although I acknowledge the decorum of humility, squint and observe a wonder!

SL: You *should* hold consistency a lark; however, you do know this contraption employs light and mirrors?

D: Plus a filter. And I know you find voice-over hackneyed; therefore, in short: a black dot slowly transits a yellow disk.

SL: I can listen to your lips and to my humming mind, so continue while I think of Holst's "The Bringer of Peace."

D: If I may, that's bang on the key! And I can shiver as I think of Cleopatra drifting the Cydnus with her mermaid crew.

SL: Go ahead and bring our thoughts together—nonetheless, is the cross-wired audiovisual *à propos* what the spinning basin of mercury conjures?

D: You understand catharsis holds no interest and is a giving up?

SL: Yes. Proceed.

D: Morns and eves, eves and morns, rays bounce off her from elsewhere than her.

SL: I'm with you, keep on, I just want to adjust a small surface I brought ...

D: Now, as her far hemisphere returns rays to their origin, her near hemisphere she offers unencumbered, triumphant.

SL: Pardon! Your aversion to this glass will ease, trust me: allow your self to drown into your body, your body into your self.

D: I know

SL: Though you perhaps know this word or that, try these: stream entry.

Acknowledgements

Grateful acknowledgements to the editors of the following journals, in which pieces from this book first appeared:

Burning House: "ignoratio elenchi"

Cheat River Review: "synchysis" & "paradox"

Denver Quarterly: "topothesia" & "polyptoton"

New Delta Review: "antimetabole" & "tricolon"

Upstairs at Duroc: "antiphrasis," "antithesis," "non-sequitur," & "synzeugma"

About Atmosphere Press

Atmosphere Press is an independent, full-service publisher for excellent books in all genres and for all audiences. Learn more about what we do at atmospherepress.com.

We encourage you to check out some of Atmosphere's latest releases, which are available at Amazon.com and via order from your local bookstore:

Saints and Martyrs: a Novel, by Aaron Roe

The Recoleta Stories, by Bryon Esmond Butler

Voodoo Hideaway, a novel by Vance Cariaga

I Would Tell You a Secret, poetry by Hayden Dansky

A Book of Life, a novel by David Ellis

It Was Called a Home, a novel by Brian Nisun

Grace, a novel by Nancy Allen

Shifted, a novel by KristaLyn A. Vetovich

Aegis of Waves, poetry by Elder Gideon

Feast, poetry by Alexandra Antonopoulos

Because the Sky is a Thousand Soft Hurts, stories by Elizabeth Kirschner

Stronghold, a novel by Kesha Bakunin

Unwinding the Serpent, a novel by Robert Paul Blumenstein

Streetscapes, poetry by Martin Jon Porter

All or Nothing, a novel by Miriam Malach

Licorice, poetry by Liz Bruno

About the Authors

Robert Savino Oventile has published interviews, essays, and book reviews in *Postmodern Culture*, *Jacket*, *symplokē*, and *Chicago Quarterly Review*, among other journals. He is the author of *Impossible Reading: Idolatry and Diversity in Literature* and of *Satan's Secret Daughters: The Muse as Daemon* (both with the Davies Group).

Sandy Florian is the author of *Telescope* (Action Books), *The Tree of No* (Action Books), *Prelude to Air from Water* (Elixir Press), *On Wonderland & Waste* (Sidebrow Press), and *Boxing the Compass* (Noemi Press).

* 9 7 8 1 6 3 7 5 2 8 5 1 8 *